The
Portrait of a Tortoise

The Rev. Gilbert White

Mrs. Rebecca Snooke

The Portrait of a Tortoise

Extracted from the Journals & Letters of
GILBERT WHITE

With an Introduction & Notes by
SYLVIA TOWNSEND WARNER

VIRAGO

Published by VIRAGO PRESS LIMITED 1981
Ely House, 37 Dover Street, London W1X 4HS
First published by Chatto & Windus Limited 1946

Printed in Great Britain by
Butler and Tanner Limited,
Frome and London

British Library Cataloguing in Publication Data

White, Gilbert
    Portrait of a tortoise.
    1. Natural History – England – Selborne
    I. Title   II. Townsend Warner, Sylvia
    500.9′422′74   QH138.S4
    ISBN 0-86068-218-8

Contents

Bibliography

Journals of Gilbert White, edited by Walter Johnson, F.G.S. 1931

The Life and Letters of Gilbert White of Selborne, by Rashleigh Holt-White. 1901

The Natural History and Antiquities of Selborne & A Garden Kalendar, edited by R. Bowdler Sharpe, L.L.D. 1900

The Natural History of Selborne, edited by E. M. Nicholson. 1929

A Modern Herbal, by M. Grieve, F.R.H.S. 1931

Editor's note, 1946

The war-time hibernation of MSS. has made it impossible to consult the original texts. For the same reason I have not been able to ascertain how and when Timothy the Tortoise's carapace came into the ownership of the British Museum of Natural History.

Publisher's note, 1981

We now know that Timothy died in 1794 and that his carapace was preserved. In 1836 it was in the possession of Mrs. Christopher, the great-niece of Gilbert White, who presented it to the British Museum of Natural History on 17 April 1853.

There is now some doubt as to whether the portrait of the Reverend Gilbert White on page ii is an authentic likeness.

Introduction

'YOUNG Hirundines cluster on the trees. Harvest bugs bite the ladies.'

If one is a lady this record of August 14, 1790, may seem a little heartless in its serene objectivity. But a naturalist penned it. A child of his most social century, Gilbert White, Curate of Selborne in Hampshire, complied with his social obligations, whether as friend, host, or member of the White family (descendants of the *Jutae* or *Viti* to whom King Ina gave a grant of settlement). There were gifts of pheasants, cucumbers, and melons; there were tea-parties at the Hermitage (his gothic summerhouse on Selborne Hanger) where Brother Harry, cowled and bearded, 'appeared to great advantage' as the Hermit; there were supper-parties when 'at one in the morn the gentlemen and us changed Caps and wigs and several minuets were danced'; there were hospitalities to brothers and sisters, nephews and nieces ('I have just ceiled and am fitting up a garret for any young person I may have with me'); there was the over-seeing of stockings being knitted locally for Brother Thomas, the finding of maid-servants for Niece Mary, and later the charge of Mary's baby who came down with his nurse to Selborne and was referred to as The Learned Pig. But through this land-scape of Conversation Pieces Gilbert White's private love-affair with Nature runs like a chalk-stream river, pellucid, tranquil, and irresistible. And so when he opens his Naturalist's Journal and sets down the outstanding events of August 14, 1790, the ladies ('Sister Barker, and nieces,

Mary and Eliz : ') take their place in the realm of nature, rolled round in earth's diurnal course with the harvest bugs and the Hirundines.

But perfect objectivity is difficult to achieve, even by a naturalist. The harvest bugs and their complementary ladies lacked the compelling charm of the Hirundines— the charm of mystery. Harvest bugs (' an insect which is very troublesome and teasing, getting into people's skins, especially those of ladies and children, and raising tumours which itch intolerably ') ' prevail only in the hot months of summer.' Ladies, on the other hand, having made some seasonal variations in their plumage, are about at all times of year. But whether the Hirundines migrated during the winter or whether they hibernated was a matter of debate ; and to his life's end Gilbert White watched and wondered, seeking, and seemingly on the brink of finding, and never finding, an unequivocal proof of hibernation. A hundred years before him Henry Wotton had written of ' the swift pilgrim's well-daubed nest.' Not till over a hundred years after Gilbert White had looked his last at a swallow was it definitely established that swallows from England had wintered in S. Africa. Between Wotton (for that matter, Shakespeare too) with their carefree poet's guess-right, and the final confirmation of scientific ornitho- logy, the tide of opinion had flowed towards hibernation —in Gilbert White's time so strongly that it collected and carried along with it a considerable amount of irrefut- able evidence. English naturalists favoured the belief of land-hibernation, and sent the swallows, swifts, and martins underground into burrows and sandbanks, or into hollow trees or the crannies of buildings. A Reverend Mr

Conway of Flintshire said he had looked down into a lead-mine and seen ' numbers of swallows clinging to the timbers of the shafts, seemingly asleep.' Near Whitby some sportsmen, digging out a fox, found ' whole bushels of swallows in a torpid condition.' Other naturalists in Northern Europe preferred to send the swallows under water. ' Dr Wallerius, the celebrated Swedish chemist,' declared he had seen swallows ' assembling on a reed, till they were all immersed and went to the bottom ; this being preceded by a dirge of a quarter of an hour's length ' ; and this theory was majestically supported by Dr Johnson : ' a number of them conglobulate together by flying round and round, and then all in a heap throw themselves under water and lie in the bed of a river.' [1]

[1] E. M. Nicholson, in his Introduction to the *Nat. Hist. of Selborne* (1929) remarks that it is a striking fact that the majority of naturalists supporting migration were ' very out-of-date seventeenth-century men.' This seems just about what one would expect if one takes into consideration the way thinking varies from one generation to another. ' To us it seems more probable that they fly away into hot Countries, viz, Egypt, Aethiopia, &c.,' says the seventeenth-century Willughby, in his forthright seventeenth-century way ; and adds that Herodotus ' witnesseth, they abide all the year in Egypt, understand it of those that are bred there (saith Aldrovandus) for those that are bred with us only fly thither to winter.' Bacon's materialism had taught the seventeenth century this confident approach to probabilities. By Gilbert White's day the Age of Reason had set in, and thought proceeded more cautiously, supporting itself by analogy instead of laying violent hands on Herodotus. By analogy with known hibernants, swallows also must be supposed to hibernate. By analogy with mankind (the Age of Reason was singularly self-regarding) some

[9]

Refusing to be immersed with Wallerius, Gilbert White does not seem to have been perfectly convinced in favour of hibernation either. But there is no doubt he hoped to be convinced. As he was what one might call a naturalistic naturalist, relying on his own observations, and as there are always some hirundines who delay their departure or arrive individualistically early, it is no wonder that he found himself observing what seemed to be evidence that swallows wintered in England. Torpidity, that strange power of passing the winter months with every faculty except the minute thread of solstitial consciousness suspended, must also be observed. 'At the Black-Bear inn in Reading there is a stream in the garden which runs under the stables ... Now all the summer this is full of carps, which roll about and are fed by travellers. When the cold weather comes, these fishes withdraw under the stables, and are invisible for months : during which period, I conclude, they must sleep. Thus the inhabitants of the water, as well as of the air and the earth, retire from the severity of winter.' Heaven and earth and the waters under the earth, all had something relevant to say about swallows ; and it was with swallows in mind that Gilbert White first began to be interested in the subject of this biography : ' Timothy, Mrs Snooke's old tortoise.'

swallows might be strong enough to fly to Africa, but the weakly or the late-fledged birds must remain behind. By a comprehensive exercise of the powers of reason, swallows, not strong enough to fly to a warm climate from Northern Europe, and equally not strong enough to spend the winter in frozen ground, must go under water.

' A land tortoise, which has been kept for thirty years in a little walled court belonging to the house where I am now visiting, retires under ground about the middle of November, and comes forth again about the middle of April.' It is thus, at the close of Letter vii to Daines Barrington, after some discursive remarks about birds and ornithologists, that Timothy first steals into public notice. The house where Gilbert White was visiting was at Ringmer in Sussex, and belonged to Mrs Rebecca Snooke, a widow, and his paternal aunt. The date of the letter is October 8, 1770. Gilbert White was fifty, Mrs Snooke seventy-six, and Timothy supposedly nearing his fortieth year. But here we are at once in the realm of supposition, and I do not see how we can emerge from it. In a letter of 1784, addressed to a young lady called Miss Heckey Mulso, Gilbert White, pretending to write in the person of Timothy, asserts that he (Timothy) ' was born in the year 1734 in the Province of Virginia.' Clearly, the choice of this date must be arbitrary, though Gilbert White had been pleased to persuade himself of it, since in a letter of the same year, written to his niece Mary White, he refers to Timothy as ' so old a domestic, who has behaved himself in so blameless a manner in the family for near fifty years.' Admitting, then, that it is not possible to establish the date of Timothy's birth, we must content ourselves with the account (also contained in the letter to Miss Mulso) of how Timothy first became connected with the White family on its distaff side ; which is, that somewhere around 1740 Mr Snooke visited the harbour town of Chichester, where he bought a tortoise from a sailor for half a crown, carried it back to Ringmer, and christened it Timothy. After this impetuous act Mr Snooke lost interest in his purchase, and Timothy, put into the little walled court, became to all intents and purposes Mrs Snooke's tortoise.[1]

Just as the ladies were complementary to the harvest bugs Mrs Rebecca Snooke is preserved for us in her nephew's writings as the owner of some Scotch Pines in which Crossbills appeared, ponds in which he observed ' vast spiders, which dive and conceal themselves on the undersides of plants,' a horse that was struck by lightning, and the subject of this biography. From family papers we learn that in the summer of 1763, being then newly a widow, she was a guest at Selborne, took part in the tea-party which was entertained by the Hermit, and witnessed the minuets when the gentlemen and ladies changed caps and wigs; and that in her eightieth year, having just recovered from a serious attack of gout, she rode out in her chaise in the month of December. Her nephew visited her regularly, and from his *Naturalist's Journal* other facts emerge, peripheral to Mrs Snooke, but nevertheless very much to her credit.

' Fern-owls haunt Mrs Snooke's orchard in autumn.'

' Mrs Snooke has gathered in all her apples, & pears : her fruit is finely flavoured in such hot years. Mrs Snooke's black grapes begin to ripen. No wasps here. The distress in this place for want of water is very great : they have few deep wells in this dry loam : & the little pits & ponds are all dry : so the neighbourhood all come for water to Mrs Snooke's pond.'

To Timothy, secluded in the little walled court, the orchard and the ponds were not significant. But the

[1] He was not the only Ringmer tortoise. See Appendix ii.

[12]

nature of the soil is a matter of concern to all self-burying animals. ' Ringmer soil is not clay on top but brick-loam : bears good apples, pears, & grapes. Clay under, which holds water like a dish.' Gilbert White usually visited Ringmer in autumn, but in 1773 he was there in December, and realised the inconveniencies of a clay substratum. ' The tortoise in Mrs Snooke's garden . . . lies in a wet border in mud & mire : with it's back bare.'

This is an affecting picture : but the Ringmer soil must be blamed for it, not Mrs Snooke. Mrs Snooke was very kind to Timothy. She fed him with her own hands, and studied his tastes. He ate of her kidney-beans and of her cucumbers. As for the little walled court, it was not the sort of prison-yard the words might suggest. It had a border in it : in the December of 1773 a wet border, but nevertheless a flower border, for in the Letter xiii to Daines Barrington Gilbert White describes how Timothy dug his hybernaculum ' beside a great tuft of hepaticas.' In this same letter Gilbert White tells his correspondent not only of Mrs Snooke's kindness to Timothy but also of Timothy's distinguishing affection for Mrs Snooke. ' I was much taken with it's sagacity in discerning those that do it kind offices : for, as soon as the good old lady comes in sight who has waited on it for more than thirty years, it hobbles towards it's benefactress with aukward alacrity ; but remains inattentive to strangers.'

Mrs Snooke's attentions to Timothy were not only of the kidney-bean and cucumber kind. She found him interesting—perhaps even taught her nephew to follow suit. It was probably at Gilbert White's request that she

kept him posted as to Timothy's winter retirements and
vernal reappearances; but the entries in White's *Journals*
based on her reports are not mere bald statements that
Timothy has gone under ground, Timothy is up and about
again: they show that she observed him closely and
sympathetically. 'Mrs Snooke's tortoise, after it had
been buried more than a month, came forth & wandered
round the garden in a disconsolate state, not knowing
where to fix on a spot for it's retreat.' In 1777 it was
Mrs Snooke's sharp eye that caught Timothy in the act of
supplying a most compelling (though erroneous) piece of
corroborative evidence for the hibernation of swallows.
Gilbert White thought so much of it that he put it in the
forefront of his Letter xxxvi to Daines Barrington.

'Dear Sir. You cannot but remember that the twenty-
sixth and twenty-seventh of last March were very hot days;
so sultry that every one complained and were restless under
those sensations to which they had not been reconciled by
gradual approaches.

'This sudden summer-like heat was attended by many
summer coincidences; for on those two days the thermometer rose to sixty-six in the shade; many species of
insects revived and came forth; some bees swarmed in
this neighbourhood; the old tortoise, near Lewes in
Sussex, awakened and came forth out of it's dormitory;
and, what is most to my present purpose, many house-
swallows appeared and were very alert in many places,
and particularly at Cobham, in Surrey.

'But as that short warm period was succeeded as well
as preceded by harsh weather, with frequent frosts and ice,
and cutting winds, the insects withdrew, the tortoise re-

[14]

tired again into the ground, and the swallows were seen no more until the tenth of April.'

Three years later Mrs Snooke died, aged eighty-six, and Gilbert White, travelling to Ringmer for her funeral, was noting along the way that no turnips were to be seen, and that 'Chaffinches sing but in a shorter way than in Hants.' Leaving Ringmer he took with him 'Mrs Snooke's old tortoise, Timothy, which she valued much, & had treated kindly for near 40 years. When dug out of it's hybernaculum, it resented the Insult by hissing.'

Thus a valued family friend passed from the ownership of one generation to another, and exchanged the clay-bottomed brick-loam of Ringmer for the black malm of Selborne. But this was not the only change. A change of mind becomes perceptible in Gilbert White's *Journal.* Timothy is no longer studied as an accessory to swallows. He begins to be studied as a personality.

During the summer of 1780 Gilbert White . . . but the words of today, concentrated, doted, and so on, are too lavish and too indiscriminate for the circumstances : one must revert to the language of his date and say that during the summer of 1780 Gilbert White was exceedingly attentive to his tortoise. Timothy was watched, Timothy was weighed. He was put into a tub of water to ascertain if he could swim (he could not). He was called to loudly through a speaking-trumpet, 'but did not seem to regard the noise.' His excrements were examined, his choice of food recorded. There is a note of rising triumph in these successive entries.

'*July 19.* Timothy picks out the hearts & stems of Coss-lettuce, holding the outer leaves back with his feet.

[15]

' *July 24.*   Tortoise eats endive and poppies.
' *July 27.*   Tortoise eats goose-berries.'

Small wonder that during the course of the summer Timothy's weight increased by eleven ounces.

In the second week of September—the peaches were ripening, and Gilbert White had just gathered his Bergamot pears—the *Journal* announces : ' The motions of Timothy the tortoise are much circumscribed : he had taken to the border under the fruit-wall, & makes very short excursions : he sleeps under a Marvel of Peru.'   This, of course, was just a preliminary sleep, a mere closing of the eyes for better meditation ; for a week later comes the experiment with the speaking-trumpet, and the reassuring entry on the following day that Timothy eats heartily.   But autumn was coming, and there is a late flock of house-martins, and Gilbert White is in high hopes ' that this late flock at least will not withdraw into warmer climes, but that they will lie dormant among the low beechen oaken shrubs ' (this entry, though nothing to do with Timothy, is interesting because it shows Gilbert White in a mid-way frame of mind), and ' men put their hogs up a fatting,' and Timothy, ' who is placed under a hen-coop near the fruit-wall, scarce moves at all.'   And Gilbert White, like the good host he is, has turned his mind to that hospitable preoccupation : how to ensure that his tortoise should spend a comfortable winter night.

The second half of the eighteenth century brought great changes to the English garden, new elements of informality, vistas, and romance.   To Gilbert White with his love for ' outlets,' evergreens, and ' annuals in the basons down the field,' the little walled court at Ringmer, survival of the mode of Mrs Snooke's youth, must have seemed very poky and unenterprising. To Timothy, on the other hand, the Selborne garden may well have seemed rather draughty. But apart from the draughtiness inseparable from English Picturesque, Gilbert White was justified in thinking (as the *Journal* so clearly shows he did think) that Timothy's change of residence was greatly to Timothy's advantage : affording him more scope for curiosity, more room for exercise, and a free run among the vegetables (at Ringmer he had to wait for Mrs Snooke to bring him his salads). With the oncome of winter Gilbert White feels even more reason to emphasise the superior amenities of Selborne. ' Timothy lies in the border under the fruit-wall, in an aspect where he will enjoy the warmth of the sun, & where no wet can annoy him : a hen-coop over his back protects him from dogs, &c. At Ringmer he used to lay himself up in a wet swampy border : indeed he had no choice.'

But in the following winter Timothy, now having choice, behaved rather oddly ; having been put to bed as before in the border under the fruit-wall, on November 8 ' the tortoise came out of his coop, & has buried himself in the laurel-hedge.' Perhaps he disliked the coop. Perhaps the soil of the fruit-wall border, being, as Gilbert White boasted, ' very light and mellow,' did not give him a sufficiently quilted sensation to ensure the proper depth of slumber. Perhaps, like many celebrated characters, he preferred to sleep austerely. Perhaps he yearned for something more like the sleeping conditions he had known for near forty years. If it was damp he wanted, he got it. For on March 28, 1782, ' Poor Timothy was flooded in his hybernaculum amidst the laurel-hedge : &

[17]   B

might have been drowned, had not his friend Thomas come to his assistance & taken him away.'

Timothy's friend Thomas was Gilbert White's friend, gardener, and factotum, Thomas Hoar. And with this introduction of Thomas we must pause to remark that he was a very unwonted kind of gardener. Even the carnivorous American tortoises are mistrusted by gardeners. Timothy, for all that the sailor said, was a Mediterranean tortoise ; and a vegetarian. The *Journals* show that the Selborne garden was a very proper sort of garden, growing fruit, flowers, and delicate vegetables, well-loved and highly cultivated ; yet Timothy had a free run of it. We find him asleep in the shade of the monk's rhubarb, or skulking among the carrots and cabbages ; he travels about the garden, in the months of high summer he traverses all the garden by six in the morning, he crops the daisies and walks to the fruit-wall border to browse the lettuces, he eats much, he is very voracious, he spoils the lettuce under the fruit-wall but will not touch the Dutch while he can get at any Coss lettuce. And all this takes place without any apparent remonstrance from Thomas Hoar, who not only rescues Timothy from drowning but himself supplies Gilbert White, then visiting in London, with the interesting detail that Timothy prefers Coss lettuce. If Timothy had been the only thorn in Thomas's pillow, Thomas's tolerance would still be remarkable. But it was not so. Thomas had many other things to endure. Mice devoured the crocuses, hares got in and nibbled off the pinks, and on one occasion a strange dog ate the apricots.

To return to Timothy. Having been rescued from

drowning under the laurel-hedge Timothy went back to the fruit-wall border and the hen-coop for the winter of 1782–83. But it was for the last time. In the autumn of 1783 he again asserted himself, and made his hybernaculum under the laurel-hedge. The hard winter of 1784–85 he also spent in that vicinity, ' under the wall-nut tree, among the dead leaves,' and so for the three winters following. In the spring of 1789 ' Timothy heaves up the sod under which he is buried,' (which suggests a different site, since the earth under a hedge is not usually grassed enough to be termed sod, and noting previous emergences from under the laurel-hedge Gilbert White says, *heaves up the earth*). Be that as it may, he is back in the laurel-hedge for the winter of 1790–91 ; but in December 1791 he ' laid himself up under the hedge against Benham's yard in a very comfortable, snug manner : a thick tuft of grass shelters his back, & he will have the warmth of the winter sun.' During the hard winter of 1784 (when Gilbert White's parlour-cat ' was so electric, that had a person stroked her, and been properly insulated, the shock might have been given to a whole circle of people '—which would have afforded her a great deal of quiet satisfaction, no doubt) the laurel-hedge suffered considerably, and Thomas Hoar was set to shake the snow off the evergreens ; and if this became a routine during the spell of snowy winters which followed it is possible that Timothy, discommoded by the vibrations of Thomas's cold stamping feet, may have moved to the hedge against Benham's yard for the sake of a little peace and quiet.[1]

[1] I hope this enquiry into Timothy's dormitories is not out of proportion. Antiquarians comment on beds where Queen

But these migrations from the blue bedroom to the brown bedroom were not Timothy's only assertions of personality. Twice he left the garden altogether. ' May 22, 1784. We have lost poor Timothy, who, being always in a great bustle in such hot weather, got out, we suppose, at the wicket, last Thursday; and is wandered we know not whither. Thomas is much discomposed at this elopement; and has—

> . . . *made as great a coil as*
> *Stout Hercules for loss of Hylas.*
> *He has forced the hangers to repeat*
> *The accent of his sad regret :*
> *And Echo from the hollow ground*
> *His doleful wailings to resound.'*

(Thomas presumably had forgotten the experiment with the speaking-trumpet; or his feelings as a friend overcame his natural philosophy.)   ' But to be serious, I should be very sorry to lose so old a domestic, who has behaved himself in so blameless a manner in the family for near fifty years.'

A postscript to this letter to Niece Mary adds, ' May 24. No Timothy to be found.'   In a letter of June 12 Mary is told of Timothy's return.   ' After Timothy had been lost eight days, he was found in the little field short of the pound-field.   He had conceived a notion of much satisfaction to be found in the range of the meadow, and Baker's hill; and that beautiful females might inhabit those vast spaces, which appeared boundless in his eye.   But having

Elizabeth spent but a single night.   Timothy spent from four to five months in his beds.

wandered 'til he was tired, and having met with nothing but weeds, and coarse grass, and solitude, he was glad to return to the poppies, and lettuces, and the other luxuries of the garden.'

One can be fanciful in a letter, especially in a letter to a young lady. 'Mrs Snooke's old tortoise' has assumed a new aspect, he is a social being, and part of the Entertainments of Selborne; another Hermit, as it were. During this same summer Miss Heckey Mulso,[1] after a visit to Selborne, wrote a letter in verse addressed to Timothy, 'which, with great labour, and pains, he answered in prose.' This is the autobiographical letter, or Pseudo-Timothy, from which we have the account of how he was bought at Chichester for half a crown. It tells, too, that when Timothy was weighed he was put in the grocer's scales, 'where I sprawl about to the great diversion of the shop-keeper's children,' and that it was a Selborne repartee, to quote from Dryden's Ode on Saint Cecilia's Day, how

> ' *Timotheus placed on high*
> *Amidst the tuneful quire,*
> *With flying fingers touched the lyre.*'

The tortoise of the Pseudo-Timothy is a poor Punchinello of an animal, not comparable to the Timothy of the *Journals*. 'Timothy, contrary to his usual practice, lies out all day in the rain.' Yet a true likeness of Timothy should include at least an impression of Timothy's master; and a letter of 1786, poised between the objectivity of the *Journals* and the benign friskings of a host, vignettes the

[1] Niece and name-child of Mrs Chapone ' who, in defiance of prejudice and fashion, made the archbishop a good man '.

man and his reptile—the hot-blooded creature, for all its observations, christianity, powers of expression and knowledge of literature, seeming slightly embarrassed in confronting the impregnable mystery of what was going on, coldly and in silence, under that carapace. ' The summer-like weather of last Friday fetched out Timothy. There is somewhat very forlorn and abject in that creature's first appearance after a profound slumber of five months. When a man first rouses himself from a deep sleep, he does not look very wise : but nothing can be more squalid and stupid than our friend, when he first comes crawling out of his hybernacula ; so that some farther lines of Dryden's Ode (written he supposes on purpose to ridicule tortoises) might well be applyed to him :—

> ' *Has rais'd up his head,*
> *As awak'd from the dead :*
> *And amaz'd he stares around.*'

' Written he supposes on purpose to ridicule tortoises.' Is it Gilbert White and Timothy or is it Monsieur Bergeret and Riquet ? Not all the beef and the bullying, not all those deplorable importees from Hanover, can smother the French accent of eighteenth-century English culture.

The midsummer weather of 1787 again transported Timothy ' beyond the bounds of his usual gravity. He was missing for some days, but found at last near the upper malt-house.' The following summer he was ' shut-up in the brew-house to prevent an escape ' ; and I suspect that a similar confinement befell him in 1789, as the entry ' Timothy begins to travel about, & be restless ' is not followed by any record of where he strayed to that time.

[22]

But ten years have passed since Timothy was brought in a box from Ringmer and buried in Selborne earth, and 'heaved up the mould, & walked twice down to the bottom of the long walk to survey the premises.' Though in the space of a decade affection may deepen, attention may wander, must wander; for while naturalists grow old Nature still replenishes, continually proffering new objects for investigation or challenging with familiar objects insufficiently observed. There are, for instance, trees. In 1790 Gilbert White began to correspond with Robert Marsham of Stratton Strawless in Norfolk, the arboriculturalist. The *Journal* for that year and the next contains many notes on trees, their girth and their age. There is the Fern Owl. Fern-owls haunted Mrs Snooke's orchard in autumn, they are no novelty; but having at last published the *Natural History of Selborne* Gilbert White is maturing a treatise on the Fern-owl, or Churn-owl, or Eve-jar—a bird that Robert Marsham also keeps his eye on. 'Sir, you know the Fern-owl is one of the Spring Birds, and appears here as the latest comer. I used to have many in my Woods; but since the long and severe winter of '88 I have had very few. Is not this a presumptive proof of their torpidity? and that they were destroyed by the severity of the Season?' And always there are the Hirundines, the problem of their behaviour still unsolved. Do they lay themselves up and become torpid, do they fly off to winter 'under the warm and sheltery shores of Gibraltar and Barbary'? 'The cats brought in a dead house-martin from the stable. I was in hopes at first sight that it might have been in a torpid state; but it was decayed, & dry.' In April 1793

'Thomas Knight, a sober hind,' told how he had seen 'several Bank Martins playing in & out, and hanging before some nest-holes in a sand-hill, where these birds usually nestle. This incident confirms my suspicions, that this species of Hirundo is the first to be seen of any;' and gives great reason to suppose 'that they do not leave their wild haunts at all, but are secreted amidst the clefts, & caverns of those abrupt cliffs . . . and, like bats and flies, have been awaked by the influence of the Sun, amidst their secret latebrae, where they have spent the uncomfortable foodless months in a torpid state, & the profoundest of slumbers.' Five days after Thomas Knight's report Timothy comes forth, and weighs 6 lbs. $5\frac{1}{2}$ oz. As a witness to profound slumbers Timothy could not be bettered; but he is only a tortoise, and in 'the dark but curious business of migration' his witness may be vain.

The spring of 1793, the last spring, unfolds. On May 2 it is 'sad, blowing, wintry weather. I think I saw a house-martin.' On May 13 'the fern-owl returns, & chatters in the hanger,' and the following day 'Timothy travels about the garden.' In the third week of May 'Timothy eats much,' and the white pippin blooms so abundantly that the weeding-woman swept up a bushel-basket of fallen petals, 'and yet that tree still seems covered with bloom.' But in spite of the blossom, it is a cold spring, 'so cold that no species of Hirundine makes any advance towards building, & breeding.' On the First of June 'Timothy is very voracious: when he can get no other food he eats grass in the walks.'

The spring had been cold and dry, and there was no sign of rain. In such a season a gardener naturally defends his greenstuff, his lettuces, Dutch or Coss (the Dutch are the hardier), in the fruit-wall border. Apparently Timothy's friend Thomas had done something in the way of netting or fencing and Timothy, voraciously travelling about the garden, found himself foiled by Thomas's contrivances, and reduced to browsing the grassed walks. The drought continued into midsummer. When the rows of large kidney-beans were sown ' the ground was so hard that it required much labour to render it fit to receive the seed.' The Provence Roses bloomed, the Dame's Violets were very fine, the Ten Weeks Stocks, that had come into bloom a month earlier, were still in full beauty. But flowers are hardy gipsies compared with vegetables, and will flaunt their way through a drought that intimidates cabbages. That rather sinister entry about Timothy eating the grass in the walks is surely only incidental to a dry season.

But it is the last we hear of him. On June 15 Gilbert White made the last entry in his *Journal* and on June 26 he died ; being buried, in accordance with his wish, not in the family vault but out of doors.

Timothy is said to have died in the spring of the following year. Perhaps the piety of family sentiment has antedated his demise, and the *ob. 1794* may be as much an intrusion of human caprice as the *nat. 1734* of the Pseudo-Timothy. The sailor who sold him to Mr Snooke, and who is, presumably, the original authority for that *nat. 1734* need not, I think, be taken very seriously. There is no reason why he should have known that Timothy was then about ten years old and every reason (since he was selling him) to assert it, for clearly Mr Snooke would prefer to buy a tortoise with a good expectation of life. On the other hand, between 1789 and 1793 Timothy's weight seems to have been going down, and this might betoken the decline of old age. The where of his death is better substantiated than the when : he must have died in the garden at Selborne, since his carapace was preserved, and is now in the British Museum of Natural History. Though Timothy is an exceptionally well-documented reptile he retains some tortoise-like privacy, he keeps his age to himself. 'And all the powerful Kings, and all the beautiful Queenes of this world, were but as a bed of flowers, some gathered at six, some at seaven, some at eight, all in one Morning, in respect of this Day.' And in respect of tortoises, if John Donne had preached a funeral sermon for a tortoise he might well have said that some complete sixty, some seventy, and some a hundred stanzas of their unobtrusive Hymn to the Sun.

TIMOTHY'S CARAPACE.

The Portrait of a Tortoise

I

IN piecing together these extracts from the *Journals* I have allowed myself to include some passages which do not directly refer to Timothy. Sometimes there is a perceptible good reason for such inclusions; weather, for instance, means a great deal to a tortoise. Though swallows and their kind mean nothing to a tortoise they meant a great deal to the Journalist; lovers of Gilbert White will allow me the swallows, and such entries as that for March 26, 1789, which show his faithful observation of nature, and his power—like that of some Chinese artist—of conveying a whole landscape with a few strokes. But in a few inclusions, such as the astonished bantams and the concatenation in a Naturalist's mind of the fertility of the polyanthus and of the White family, I have just given way to personal liking. Readers who know the *Journals* will be astonished at my moderation.

· ✳ ·

1771

Nov. 1. Mrs Snooke's tortoise begins to scrape an hole in the ground in order for laying up.

Nov. 2. Mrs Snooke's tortoise begins to dig in order to hide himself for the winter. The vale of Bramber, & the river enveloped in a vast fog: the downs were clear.

Nov. 10. Tortoise comes out in the sun about noon, but soon returns to his work of digging a hole to retire into.

Nov. 15. Tortoise at Ringmer had not finish'd his hybernaculum, being interrupted by the sunny weather, which tempted him out. (1)

1772

May 22. Tortoise eats.   Fly-catcher appears, and builds.
May 23. The Ringmer-tortoise came forth from its hybernaculum on the *6th* of April, but did not appear to eat 'til May the *5th* : it does not eat but on hot days.   As far as I could find it has no perceptible pulse. (2)
May 30. Tortoise eats all day.   In Mrs Snooke's ponds are vast spiders, which dive & conceal themselves on the underside of plants, lying on the water : perhaps aranea aquatica Linn : urinatoria.   The swallow seems to be the only bird which washes itself as it flies, by dropping into the water.

1773

Dec. 2.   The tortoise in Mrs Snooke's garden went under ground Novr 21 : came out on the *30th* for one day, & retired to the same hole : lies in a wet border in mud & mire : with it's back bare. (3)
Dec. 17. Mrs Snooke's tortoise, after it had been buried more than a month, came forth & wandered round the garden in a disconsolate state, not knowing where to fix on a spot for it's retreat. (4)

1775

Mar. 21. Mrs Snooke's old tortoise came out of the ground, but in a few days buried himself as deep as ever.
Apr. 17. Mrs Snooke's tortoise came out of the ground the second time, for the summer. (5)

[28]

Aug. 7. Timothy, Mrs Snooke's old tortoise has been kept full 30 years in the court before the house, weighs six pounds three quarters & one ounce. It was never weighed before, but seems to be much grown since it came. (1)

1776

Aug. 20. Timothy, the tortoise weighs just six pounds three quarters & two ounces & an half: so is increased in weight, since Aug. 1775, just one ounce & an half. (2)
Aug. 28. The tortoise eats voraciously: is particularly fond of kidney-beans. Vast halo round the moon.
Nov. 20. Mrs Snooke's old tortoise at Ringmer went under ground. (3)

1777

Mar. 26 & 27. Two sultry days; Mrs Snooke's tortoise came forth out of the ground; but retired again to it's hybernaculum in a day or two, & did not appear any more for near a fortnight. Swallows appeared also on the same days, & withdrew again: a strong proof this of their hiding. (4)
Sept. 11. Mrs Snooke's tortoise devours kidney-beans & cucumbers in a most voracious manner: swallows it's food almost whole. *Foot note.* Timothy the tortoise weighed six pounds 3 quarters, 2 oun: & an half: so is not at all increased in weight since this time last year. The scales were not very exact. (5)

1778

Oct. 2. Timothy, the old tortoise, weighed six pounds, & eleven ounces averdupoise. (6)

1779

Oct. 23. Timothy, the old tortoise at this house, weighs 6 pounds 9 ounces & an half averdupoise.   It weighed last year, Oct. 2, an ounce & an half more.   But perhaps the abstemious life that it lives at this season may have reduced it's bulk : for tortoises seem to eat nothing for some weeks before they lay-up.   However this enquiry shows, that these reptiles do not, as some have imagined, continue to grow as long as they live.   This poor being has been very torpid for some time ; but it does not usually retire under ground 'til the beginning of next month. (1)

Nov. 25. Mrs Snooke's old tortoise retired under the ground. (2)

Nov. 28. The ground is glutted with water.

1780

Mar. 6. Sky-larks mount & sing.

Mar. 8. Mrs Snooke dyed, aged 86.

Mar. 14. Chaffinches sing but in a shorter way than in Hants.

Mar. 15. Mrs Snooke was buried. (3)

Mar. 17. Brought away Mrs Snooke's old tortoise, Timothy, which she valued much, & had treated kindly for near 40 years.   When dug out of it's hybernaculum, it resented the Insult by hissing.

Mar. 20. We took the tortoise out of it's box, & buried it in the garden : but the weather being warm it heaved up the mould, & walked twice down to the bottom of the long walk to survey the premises. (4)

Mar. 21. The tortoise is quite awake, & came-out all day long : towards the evening it buried itself in part.

Mar. 25. Sowed carrots, parsneps, planted potatoes. Ground works well. Tortoise sleeps.

Mar. 28. The tortoise put out his head in the morning.

Mar. 30. Tortoise keeps close.

Apr. 5. The frost injured the bloom of the wall-trees: covered the bloom with boughs of ivy.

Apr. 7. Tortoise keeps still in its hole.

Apr. 15. Cucumbers swell. Tortoise sleeps on. Radishes are drawn.

Apr. 21. The tortoise heaves up the earth, & puts out it's head.

Apr. 22. Tortoise comes-forth & walks round his coop: will not eat lettuce yet: goes to sleep at four o'clock p:m:

May 2. Tortoise marches about: eat part of a cucumber-paring.

May 10. Stormy all night. Tortoise scarce moves during this wet time.

May 11. Tortoise moves about, but does not feed yet.

May 13. After a fast of 7, or 8 months, the tortoise which in Oct. 1779 weighed six pounds 9 oun: & ½ averdupoise, weighs now only 6 pounds 4 ounces. Timothy begins to break his fast May 17 on the globe-thistle, & American willow-herb; his favourite food is lettuce, & dandelion, cucumber, & kidney-beans. (1)

May 27. Timothy the tortoise possesses a much greater share of discernment than I was aware of: & ' —is much too wise to go into a well'; for when he arrives at the haha, he distinguishes the fall of the ground, & retires with caution, or marches carefully along the edge: he delights in crawling up the flower-bank, & walking along it's verge.(2)

May 29. The tortoise shunned the heat, it was so intense.

June 1. Distant clouds, sultry, thunder-clouds. Sulphurous smell in the air. Sweet even, small shower. Strawberries blow well. Medlar shows much bloom. Honey-suckles blow. Fern-owl chatter: chur-worm jars. The tortoise shuns the intense heat by covering itself with dead grass; and does not eat 'til the afternoon.

June 5. Tortoise does not move. Tulips fade. Cinnamon-roses blow.

July 1. The red valerians, roses, iris's, corn-flags, honey-suckles, lilies, &c., make a gallant show. Most of the pinks were destroyed in the winter by the hares. We put Timothy in a tub of water, & found that he sunk gradually, and walked on the bottom of the tub: he seemed quite out of his element, & was much dismayed. This species seems not at all amphibious. Timothy seems to be the *Testudo Graeca* of Linnaeus. Dr Chandler who saw the operation, says there is a species of tortoise in the Levant that at times frequents ponds & lakes: and my Bro: John White, affirms the same of a sort in Andalusia. (1)

July 3. The tortoise weighs six pounds & three quarters averdupoise: six pds. 12 oun:

July 8. The excrement of the tortoise is hard & solid: but when that creature urines, as it often does plentifully, it voids after the water a soft white matter, much like the dung of birds of prey, which dries away into a sort of chalk-like substance.

July 10. Timothy eats voraciously; but picks out the hearts & stems of Coss-lettuce, holding the outer leaves back with his feet.

July 24. Tortoise eats endive & poppies.

July 27. Tortoise eats goose-berries.

Aug. 12. Dust flies. Gardens suffer from want of rain. Much wheat bound. Timothy, in the beginning of May, after fasting all the winter, weighed only *six pounds & four ounces* averdupoise; is now encreased to *six pounds & 15 ounces*, averdupoise.

Aug. 22. Timothy is sluggish, & scarce moves.

Sep. 10. The motions of Timothy the tortoise are much circumscribed: he has taken to the border under the fruit-wall, & makes very short excursions: he sleeps under a Marvel of Peru. (1)

Sept. 12. Timothy still feeds a little.

Sept. 17. When we call loudly thro' the speaking-trumpet to Timothy, he does not seem to regard the noise. (2)

Sept. 18. Timothy eats heartily.

Oct. 3. No ring-ouzels seen this autumn yet. Timothy very dull.

Oct. 13. The tortoise scarcely moves.

Oct. 29. Men put their hogs up a fatting. Timothy the tortoise, who in May last, after fasting all the winter, weighed only 6 pds. & four ounces; & in Aug. when full fed weighed 6 pds. & 15 ounces: weighs now 6 pds. 9 oun: & an $\frac{1}{2}$: & so he did last Octr at Ringmer. Thus his weight fluctuates, according as he fasts or abstains.

Nov. 2. Leaves fall very fast. My hedges shew beautiful lights, & shades: the yellow of the tall maples makes a fine contrast against the green hazels.

Nov. 3. Timothy, who is placed under a hen-coop near the fruit-wall, scarce moves at all.

Nov. 6. The tortoise begins to dig mould for his winter retreat: he has much moss in his coop, under which he conceals himself.

C

Nov. 7. Some snow on the ground. Many trees were stripped last night: vine-leaves begin to fall. Winter-weather.

Nov. 9. Timothy does not stir.

Nov. 13. Wheat-stubbles plow-up in fine order; green wheat comes up well. *Tortoise* goes under ground: over him is thrown a coat of moss. The border being very light & mellow, the tortoise has thrown the mould entirely over his shell, leaving only a small breatheing hole near his head. Timothy lies in the border under the fruit-wall, in an aspect where he will enjoy the warmth of the sun, & where no wet can annoy him: a hen-coop over his back protects him from dogs, &c. *Foot note.* The severity of the weather quickened Timothy's retreat: he used to stay above ground 'til about the 20th. At Ringmer he used to lay himself up in a wet swampy border: indeed he had no choice. (1)

Nov. 28. Timothy lies very snug but does not get any deeper.

1781

Feb. 11. The tortoise came-forth & continued to be alert 'til the 25*th*, & then eat some lettuce; when the weather turning very harsh he retired under the straw in his coop. (2)

Apr. 1. The tortoise came-out for two hours.

Apr. 2. Tortoise out. Timothy weighs 6 lbs. 8¾ oz. The beginning of last May he weighed only 6 lbs. 4 oz.

Apr. 3. Timothy eats heartily. The wry-neck appears & pipes.

May 8. Timothy lies close this cold weather.

July 7. Timothy the tortoise, who weighed April 2 : after fasting all the winter only *six pounds 8 oun.* & ¾ : weighs now *seven pounds*, & *one ounce* : weighed last August *six pounds*, & 15 ounces. From the encreased number of the *Swifts*, it seems as if they had brought out many of their young. About eight in the evening, Swifts get together in a large party, & course round the environs of the church, as if to teach their broods the art of flying.

July 29. Timothy comes-out but little, while the weather is so hot : he skulks among the carrots, & cabbages.

Sept. 10. Red-breasts feed on elder-berries, enter rooms, & spoil the furniture. Timothy, whose appetite is now on the decline, weighs only 7 pounds & ¾ of an ounce : at Midsummr he weighed 7 ae i oun: (1)

Sept. 14. Timothy the tortoise dull & torpid.

Oct. 24. The tortoise is very torpid, but does not bury itself.

Oct. 27. My well sinks & is very low. The tortoise begins to dig into the ground. The bat is out this warm evening.

Oct. 30. The *tortoise* retires under ground, within his coop.

Nov. 8. The *tortoise* came out of his coop, & has buried himself in the laurel-hedge. (2)

1782

Mar. 28. Poor Timothy was flooded in his hybernaculum amidst the laurel-hedge ; & might have been drowned, had not his friend Thomas come to his assistance & taken him away.

May 2. Two swifts at Nore hill passed by me at a steady rate towards this village as if they had just arrived.

May 4. Vegetation is at a stand, & Timothy the tortoise fast asleep. The trees are still naked.

May 10. The tortoise weighs 6 ae 11 oun. 2 dr. He weighed Spring 1781, 6: 8: 4 & May 1780 6: 4: o.

May 14. Tortoise eats the leaves of poppies.

June 16. This hot weather makes the tortoise so alert that he traverses all the garden by six o'clock in the morning. When the sun grows very powerful he retires under a garden-mat, or in the shelter of some cabbage ; not loving to be about in vehement heat. In such weather he eats greedily.

July 29. Fine wood-straw-berries again. A strong stream of water runs in Norton mead among the hay-cocks.

Aug. 1. Timothy the tortoise weighed seven pounds & three ounces.

Oct. 17. No baking pears. Gathered-in medlars. Dug up carrots, a good crop, but small in size. The tortoise not only gets into the sun under the fruit-wall ; but he tilts one edge of his shell against the wall, so as to incline his back to it's rays : by which contrivance he obtains more heat than if he lay in his natural position. And yet this poor reptile has never read, that planes inclining to the horizon receive more heat from the sun than any other elevation. At four P.M. he retires to bed under the broad foliage of a holyhock. He has ceased to eat for some time.

Nov. 26. The woods, & hedges are beautifully fringed with snow. Ordered Thomas carefully to beat-off the snow that lodges on the South side of the laurels & laurustines.

Nov. 27. Fierce frost. Rime hangs all day on the hanger. The hares, press'd by hunger, haunt the gardens & devour the pinks, cabbages, parsley, &c. Cats catch the **red**-breasts. Timothy the tortoise sleeps in the fruit-border under the wall, covered with a hen-coop, in which is a good armfull of straw. Here he will lie warm, secure, & dry. His back is partly covered with mould.

1783

Feb. 18. Cleaned-up the borders in the garden. Sowed radishes, & a few carrots under the fruit-wall.

Feb. 19. Men busy in plowing for pease. Timothy the tortoise awakes.

Apr. 2. Timothy, my tortoise, came-out for the first time at Selborne. Aurora bor: (1)

Apr. 17. Tortoise weighs 6 ae $11\frac{1}{4}$ oun. He begins to eat.

Apr. 18. A nightingale sings in my fields. Young rooks.

Aug. 31. Timothy begins to frequent the border under the fruit-wall for the sake of warmth.

Sept. 1. Red sunshine. Sowed a bed of Coss-lettuce.

Oct. 17. Mowed & burnt the dead grass in my fields. Rooks on the hill attended by a numerous flock of starlings. The tortoise gets under the laurel-hedge, but does not bury himself.

Oct. 29. Tortoise begins to bury himself in the laurel-hedge.

1784

Apr. 17. The buds of the vines have not swelled yet at all. In fine springs they have shot by this time two or three inches.

Apr. 19. Timothy the tortoise begins to stir : he heaves

up the mould that lies over his back. Red-start is heard at the verge of the highwood against the common.

Apr. 22. The spring backward to an unusual degree! Some swallows are come, but I see no insects except bees, & some phalaenae in the evenings. Daffodils begin to blow.

Apr. 23. Timothy the tortoise comes forth from his winter-retreat.

Apr. 29. The hoar-frost was so great that Thomas could hardly mow.

May 3. Goody hampton came to work in the garden for the summer. Timothy the tortoise weighs 6 ae 13 oun: he weighed at first coming out last year only 6 ae 11¼ oun. He eat this morning the heart of a lettuce. (1)

May 5. Cut the first cucumber, a large one.

May 15. The tortoise is very earnest for the leaves of poppies, which he hunts about after, & seems to prefer to any other green thing.

May 22. Columbine & Monkshood blow. The sycomores, & maples in bloom scent the air with a honeyed smell. Lily of the valley blows. Lap-wings on the downs.

May 28. Timothy the tortoise has been missing for more than a week. He got out of the garden at the wicket, we suppose; & may be in the fields among the grass. Timothy found in the little bean-field short of the pound-field. The nightingale, fern-owl, cuckow, & grass-hopper lark may be heard at the same time in my outlet.

Nov. 4. Timothy out. Great meteor. (2)

Dec. 2. Timothy is buried we know not where in the laurel hedge.

Dec. 6. Dismally dark : no wind with this very sinking glass.

Dec. 9. Much snow in the night. Vast snow. Snow 16 inches deep on my grass-plot : about 12 inches at an average. Farmer Hoar had 41 sheep buried in snow.

Dec. 10. Extreme frost ! ! ! yet still bright sun. At 11 one degree below zero. Thomas Hoar shook the snow carefully off from the evergreens. The snow fell for 24 hours without ceasing.

1785

Jan. 1. Much snow on the ground. Ponds frozen-up & almost dry. Moles work : cocks crow. Ground soft under the snow. No field-fares seen : no wag-tails. Evergreens miserably scorched ; even ivy, in warm aspects.

Feb. 2. The scorched laurels cast their leaves, & are almost naked.

Apr. 1. Snow hangs in the trees, & makes a perfect winter scene !

Apr. 15. Hot sun. Muddy sky. Goose-berries & honeysuckles begin to bud, & look green. My fine jasmine is dead. *Timothy* the *tortoise* roused himself from his winter-slumbers & came forth. He was hidden in the laurel-hedge under the wall-nut tree, among the dead leaves.

Apr. 18. The Cuckow is heard this day.

May 11. Severe drying exhausting drought. Cloudless days. The country all dust. Timothy the tortoise weighs 6 ae 11¾ oun. He spoils the lettuce under the fruit-wall : but will not touch the Dutch, while he can get at any coss. (1)

[39]

Sept. 28. Timothy the tortoise spends all the summer in the quarters of the kitchen-garden among the asparagus, &c. but as soon as the first frosty mornings begin, he comes forth to the laurel-hedge, by the side of which he spends the day, & retires under it at night; 'till urged by the encreasing cold he buries himself in Novr amidst the laurel-hedge.

Oct. 21. Timothy the tortoise lies in the laurel-hedge, but is not buried.

1786

Apr. 14. Timothy heaves up the mould, & comes out of his hibernacula under the wallnut-tree.

Apr. 16. Timothy the tortoise, after a fast of more than five months, weighs 6 ae. 12 oz. 11 dr.   Some snow in Shalden lanes.   Crown Imperial blows.

Apr. 23. Grass lamb.   Timothy, if you offer him some poppy leaves, will eat a little; but does not seek for food.

May 6. Great showers, & hail all round.   Showers of hail at a distance look of a silvery colour.   Rain-bow. The hanger is bursting into leaf every hour.   A progress in foliage may be discerned every morning, & again in the evening.

May 8. Pastures yellow with bloom of dandelion, & with cowslips.

May 9. Timothy, contrary to his usual practice, lies out all day in the rain.

May 15. Timothy begins to march about at 5 in the morning.

1787

Mar. 18. Timothy the tortoise heaves up the earth: he lies under the wall-nut tree.

Mar. 19. Women hoe wheat. Gossamer abounds.

Mar. 22. The tortoise comes forth from his hole.

Mar. 23. Timothy hides his head under the earth.

Mar. 27. Swallows were first seen this year at Messina in Sicily.

Mar. 28. Timothy continues to lie very close.

May 6. Timothy, the tortoise, who has just begun to eat, weighs 6 ae, 12½ oz.

May 7. The large white pippin-tree full of bloom. No house-martin seen yet!

June 5. The tortoise took his usual ramble, & could not be confined within the limits of the garden. His pursuits, which seem to be of the amorous kind, transport him beyond the bounds of his usual gravity at this season. He was missing for some days, but found at last near the upper malt-house. (1)

Aug. 26. Timothy the tortoise, who has spent the last two months amidst the umbrageous forests of the asparagus-beds, now begins to be sensible of the chilly autumnal mornings; & therefore suns himself under the laurel-hedge, into which he retires at night. He is become sluggish, & does not seem to take any food.

Aug. 31. Young hirundines cluster on the dead boughs of the walnut tree.

Oct. 9. Timothy sets his shell on edge against the sun.

Dec. 24. Deep snow. The Bantham fowls, when they were first let out, were so astonished at the snow that they flew over the house.

1788

Apr. 8. Timothy heaves up the earth.

Apr. 10. Crown Imperials blow, & stink. Much goss-amer. Bat.

Apr. 21. Timothy begins to eat: he crops the daisies, & walks down to the fruit-wall to browse on the lettuces.

Apr. 24. Grass-hopper lark whispers. Cowslips blow.

Apr. 30. Began to mow the orchard for the horses. Timothy weighs 6 ae 13 oz. 10 dr. Mole-cricket churs.

May 4. Shade the best tulips from the vehemence of the sun. Polyanths are hurried out of bloom. Vine-shoots are forward. Timothy wanders round the garden, & strives to escape: he is shut-up in the brew-house to prevent an escape.

July 5. Timothy grazes on the grass-plot. Some dishes of wood straw-berries are brought to the door.

1789

Mar. 26. Icicles hang all day. Hot-bed smokes.

Apr. 1. Rain in the night, spring-like. Crocus's make a gaudy show. Some little snow under the hedges.

Apr. 5. *Wry-neck* pipes. The smallest *uncrested wren* chirps loudly, & sharply in the hanger.

Apr. 6. Timothy the tortoise heaves up the sod under which he is buried. Daffodil blows.

Apr. 9. Brimstone butter-fly. The tortoise comes out. Dog violets blow. Summer like.

Apr. 11. White frost, sun. Timothy the tortoise weighs 6 ae. 14 oz. Dug several plots of garden ground & ground digs well. Sweet even.

Apr. 28. Timothy the tortoise begins to eat dandelion.

[42]

Apr. 29. Scarce an hirundo has been seen about this village.

May 23. White thorn blows.   The air is filled with floating willow-down.   Martins begin to build against the end of my brew-house.   Columbines blow.   Timothy the tortoise begins to travel about, & be restless.

Sept. 15. The hops at Kimbers grow dingy & lose their colour.

Sept. 16. Timothy the tortoise is very dull, & inactive, & spends his time on the border under the fruit-wall.

Sept. 18. Began to light fires in the parlors.

Nov. 6. The hermitage capped with snow. (1)

Nov. 11. The tortoise is going under ground, but not quite buried : he is in motion, & pushing himself beneath the turf.

Nov. 12. Bror & Sister Benjn left us & went to Newton. Tortoise almost covered.

1790

Feb. 27. Daffodils begin to open.

Feb. 28. Violets abound.

Mar. 4. Timothy the tortoise comes forth : he does not usually appear 'till the middle of April.

Mar. 5. The tortoise does not appear.

Mar. 17. Timothy the tortoise lies very close in the hedge.

May 9. Timothy the tortoise eats dandelion leaves & stalks : he swallows his food almost whole.

May 15. Timothy the tortoise weighs 6 ae 12 oz. 14 drs.

May 16. One polyanth-stalk produced 47 pips or blossoms. Mrs Edmund White brought to bed of a boy, who has encreased the number of my nephews & nieces, to 56.   The bloom of apples is great : the white pippin, as usual, very full.   It is a most useful tree, & always bears fruit. (1)

July 14. Tempest, & much thunder to the N.W.   Neither cucumbers, nor kidney beans, nor annuals thrive on account of the cold blowing season.   Timothy the tortoise is very dull, & spends most of his time under the shade of the vast, expanded leaves of the monk's rhubarb. (2)

Oct. 7.   Timothy the tortoise came out into the walk, & grazed.

Nov. 13. Bror & Sister Benjn left us. (3)

Nov. 15. Timothy the tortoise gone under ground in the laurel-hedge.   Paths very dry : boys play at taw on the plestor.

1791

Mar. 13. Crocus's in high glory.   Some snow under hedges.   Vast halo round the moon.

Mar. 14. Daffodil blows.   Timothy the tortoise heaves-up the earth.

Mar. 15. Sweet weather.   Mackerel.

Mar. 17. The *stone-curlew* is returned again : & was heard this evening passing over the village from the uplands down to the meadows & brooks.   Planted ½ hundred of cabbages.   Timothy comes out.

Mar. 19. Timothy hides himself again.

Mar. 23. Soft wind.   The wood-pecker laughs.

Apr. 11. Timothy the tortoise marches forth on the grass-plot and grazes.

Apr. 12. Mountain snow-drops blow.   Black thorns blossom.   Hannah White walks up to the alcove before breakfast. (4)

Apr. 15. A nightingale sings in my outlet.

June 14. White frost, dark & cold ; covered the kidney-beans with straw last night. Kidney-beans injured, & in some gardens killed. The cold weather interrupts the house-martins in their building, & makes them leave their nests unfinished. I have no martins at the end of my brew-house, as usual.

June 18. Timothy hides himself during this wintry weather.

Aug. 18. Timothy grazes. Cut 133 more cucumbers. Farmer Spencer, & Farmer Knight make each a noble wheat-rick : the crop very good, & in fine order.

Aug. 19. Sweet day, golden even, red horizon. Some what of an autumnal feel.

Sept. 13. Timothy eats voraciously.

Dec. 3. Snow covers the ground, snow shoe deep.

Dec. 5. Cut down, & covered the artichokes : covered the rhubarb plants ; & the lettuces under the fruit-wall, & the spinage lightly with straw.

Dec. 8. Timothy has laid himself up under the hedge against Benham's yard in a very comfortable, snug manner : a thick tuft of grass shelters his back, & he will have the warmth of the winter sun. (1)

1792

Mar. 16. Daffodil blows.

Mar. 23. Timothy the *tortoise* comes out. Crown imperials bud for bloom, & stink much. (2)

Mar. 26. Crocus's go off. The Kingsley miller assures me he saw a *Swallow* skimming over the meadow near the mill.

Apr. 9. Nightingale sings. *Cuckoo* is heard. Timothy the tortoise weighs 6 ae 11½ oz.

July 14. The double roses rot in the bud without blowing out : an instance this of the coldness, & wetness of the summer.

Nov. 15. Timothy comes out.

Nov. 22. Timothy comes forth.

Nov. 26. Timothy hides.

Dec. 4. Timothy is gone under a tuft of long grass, but is not yet buried in the ground.

Dec. 5. Timothy appears, & flies come-out.

1793

Mar. 14. Papilio rhamni, the brimstone butterfly, appears in the Holt. Timothy the tortoise comes forth, & weighs 6 ae. 5½ oz. (1)

Apr. 12. The *Nightingale* was heard this harsh evening near James Knight's ponds. This bird of passage, I observe, comes as early in cold cutting springs, as mild ones !

Apr. 19. Showers of hail, sleet. Gleams. Timothy, who has withdrawn himself for several days, appears.

Apr. 20. The *Cuckoo* is heard on Greatham common.

May 3. Timothy eats.

May 14. Timothy travels about the garden.

May 21. Timothy eats much.

June 1. Timothy is very voracious : when he can get no other food he eats grass in the walks.

· ✳ ·

Notes

page 28

(1) G. W. was at Ringmer Nov. 1–14. On Nov. 14 he noted in his *Journal* ' an epidemic disease among the dogs in Sussex, which proves fatal to many. They pine away, & die moping.' The dogs occupied his attention ; but on the morrow he recalled the tortoise.

(2) G. W. was at Ringmer May 22–June 3. The dates of Timothy's first appearance and first meal were supplied by Mrs Snooke.

(3) G. W. arrived at Ringmer on Dec. 2. The details of Timothy's November behaviour again supplied by Mrs Snooke.

(4) G. W. is at Selborne. The news of Timothy must have come in a letter from Mrs Snooke. On Dec. 9 G. W. records ' almost continual frost from Nov. 20.' Dec. 14 was ' dark & mild, spitting rain, great rain. Earth-worms are alert, & throw-up their casts this mild weather.' The change in the weather presumably unsettled Timothy too.

(5) This, and the previous entry, supplied by Mrs Snooke, and inserted by G. W. in the *Journal* under the appropriate dates.

page 29

(1) G. W. was at Ringmer Aug. 3–18. This is an important entry. It contains the first mention of the tortoise by name, his first recorded weight, and the length of time he had been at Ringmer.

(2) G. W. was at Ringmer Aug. 16–27.

[47]

(3) Supplied by Mrs Snooke.

(4) See *Nat. Hist. Selb.*, Letter xxxvi. Mrs Snooke supplied the information about Timothy, the swallows seem to have been hearsay. During these interesting two days G. W. was in London, and able to observe the thermometer only.

(5) G. W. at Ringmer.

(6) G. W. at Ringmer.

page 30

(1) G. W. at Ringmer.

(2) Supplied by Mrs Snooke. Though the entry for Nov. 28 refers to the state of the ground at Selborne I suspect G. W. had Timothy in mind.

(3) 'In my journey I have caught a cold, and cough; and am feverish; so I shall be glad when I am home.' Letter to Miss M. White.

(4) 'Timothy the tortoise accompanyed me from Ringmer. A jumble of 81 miles awakened him so thoroughly, that in the morning I turned him out into the garden, he walked twice the whole length of it, to take a survey of the new premises; but in the evening he retired under the mould, and is lost in the most profound slumbers; and probably may not come forth for these ten days or fortnight.' Letter to Miss M. White.

page 31

(1) Globe thistle (*Echinops*) came into English gardens in the sixteenth century. The young shoots of Willow-herb or Rosebay (*Epilobium angustifolium*) can, it is said, be eaten as a spring vegetable. Willow-herb is now a weed

in most gardens, and in blitzed London, but Gerard mentions it 'for the decking up of houses and gardens,' and G. W. 'transplanted the striped Epilobium into a fresh bason.' *Garden Kalendar*, 1759.

(2) 'Not quite a madman, though a pasty fell, And much too wise to go into a well.' Pope. *Imitations of Horace*. A haha is a sunken boundary.

page 32

(1) Timothy was a *Testude Ibera*. Dr Chandler who took part in this operation was Richard Chandler, author of *Travels in Asia Minor*, and *Travels in Greece*. See Appendix I.

page 33

(1) The phrase *Timothy the tortoise* which occurs so often in the *Journals* was not a whimsy of nomenclature. It was used to distinguish him from Timothy Turner, a farmer of the neighbourhood. Marvel of Peru (*Mirabilis Jalapa*), was one of the flowers regularly sown by G. W. in his annual bed, along with African and French Marigolds, Iroquois-Gourds, Balsams, and Pendulous Amaranths.

(2) 'It does not appear from experiment that bees are in any way capable of being affected by sounds : for I have often tried my own with a large speaking-trumpet held close to their hives, and with such an exertion of voice as would have hailed a ship at a distance of a mile, and still these insects pursued their various employments, undisturbed and without showing the least sensibility or resentment.' *Nat. Hist. Selborne*. Letter xxxviii to

D

Daines Barrington. cf. Darwin's experiment of exposing a Sensitive Plant to the bassoon.

page 34

(1) 'Timothy, your friend, retreated into his hybernaculum last week: he is laid up in the fruit border, in a dry, wholesome, sunny spot: at Ringmer he was forced to lie in a swamp.' Letter to Samuel Barker, Nov. 23.

(2) Observed and supplied by Thomas Hoar. G. W. was staying at South Lambeth at the time.

page 35

(1) ae = *librae*.

(2) 'The tortoise went under the ground in his coop, but not liking his quarters, on Nov. 8 he lifted up his coop, and came forth, and buried himself in the laurel-hedge, where he will probably be lost in the profoundest of slumbers during the uncomfortable months of winter.' Letter to Miss M. White, Nov. 13, 1781.

page 37

(1) G. W. was at South Lambeth Mar. 11–Apr. 10. 'Thomas kept the rain at Selborne.'

page 38

(1) Goody Hampton was G. W.'s weeding-woman. 'This is the person that Thomas says he likes as well as a man; and indeed excepting that she wears petticoats, and now and then has a child, you would think she was a man.' Letter to Miss M. White, Apr. 13, 1778. G. W. also refers to her as Goody Hammond.

(2) cf. Apr. 2, 1783 (for what it is worth).

page 39

(1) *Spoils* probably used in the sense of despoil. 'We have cucumbers, and a few asparagus : but Timothy has devoured most of my lettuce.' Letter to Miss M. White, May 17, 1785.

page 41

(1) Supplied by Thomas Hoar. G. W. was in London. His friend, the Rev. R. Churton, was staying at Selborne, and wrote to G. W. on June 6 : ' No Mr White, no Mrs J. White, no Mr Edmund White, no Mrs Etty ! Alas poor Selborne ! thy grotesque lanes, thy romantic vales, thy delightful walks, thy verdant hills, thy extensive prospects deserve to be honoured by other inhabitants than the philosophic Timothy in the beginning of June.' Timothy, however, was just then not so philosophic as Mr. Churton supposed.

page 43

(1) The Hermitage was G. W.'s summer-house on Selborne Hanger.

page 44

(1) ' My polyanths, which I raised from seed given me by Mrs Snooke, & sowed last spring, now make a most beautiful appearance ; many of them have large upright stems, producing many flowers, which are large, beautifully striped, & open flat.' *Garden Kalendar*. The *Garden Kalendar* also mentions ' Hepaticas, fritillarias, & winter aconites from Ringmer.' Timothy was not without the company of old friends in the Selborne garden.

(2) 'Monks rhubarb seven foot high; makes a noble appearance in bloom.' *Journal*, June 1, 1789. Monk's rhubarb (*rumex alpinus*) is, according to Culpeper's *Herbal*, ' a Dock bearing the name of Rhubarb for some purging quality therein.' On May 10, 1790, however, G. W. records, ' Made some tarts with the stalks of the leaves of the garden, or Monk's rhubarb ' and notes two days later, ' The rhubarb-tart good, & well-flavoured.' Possibly his Monk's rhubarb was some variety of Rheum after all. An alternative name for this plant is *Garden Patience*.

(3) cf. entry for Nov. 12, 1789. G. W.'s relations visited him (as he visited them) with regularity; and as one reads in the *Journals* of their arrivals and departures one insensibly comes to look on them as further examples of seasonal behaviour. Benjamin White (the publisher) was G. W.'s second brother, he married 1st Anne Yalden, 2nd Mary Yalden (widow of Anne Yalden's brother). It was brother Benjamin that G. W. visited in S. Lambeth. This ' sister Benjn ' is Mary. She appears in the frontispiece to the *Nat. Hist. Selborne*.

(4) Hannah White was Benjamin's daughter by Anne Yalden. Just as her parents appear to hibernate with Timothy, Hannah appears like Timothy to march forth and be active in Spring. The alcove was on Selborne Hanger. G. W. also called it ' the new Hermitage.'

page 45

(1) 'My tortoise was very backward this year in preparing his Hybernaculum; and did not retire until the beginning of December.' Letter to Robert Marsham,

Dec. 19, 1791. Benham was an old neighbour of G. W.'s. As early as 1769 he was supplying dung for the garden; on Feb. 4, 1791, 'Benham finished mending the hedges,' and two years later we find him impressed into a hunt for swallows. '*Apr. 6, 1793.* On the 6th of last Octr I saw many swallows hawking for flies around the Plestor, & a row of young ones, with square tails, sitting on a spar of the old ragged thatch of the empty house. This morning Dr Chandler & I caused the roof to be examined, hoping to have found some of these birds in their winter retreat; but we did not meet with any success, tho' Benham searched every hole & every breach in the decayed roof.'

(2) Timothy and the Crown Imperials had similarly coincided in 1788. Florist's catalogues are not so candid about the Crown Imperial.

page 46

(1) G. W. was visiting the Benjamin Whites at Mareland, Mar. 4–15. Perhaps Thomas Hoar took Timothy to be weighed in the grocer's scales. But cf. 'Timothy the tortoise came forth on the 15th instant, and has appeared almost every day since.' Letter to Benjamin White, Mar. 21, 1793.

The Portrait of a Tortoise

II

THE Timothy of *The Letters on the Natural History of Selborne* is at first sight a more stately and polished reptile than the Timothy of the *Journals*. A comparison of the two portraits shows that this is mainly a difference of lighting, and due to the moral and philosophical reflections which shade him in the one and not in the other.

· ☼ ·

Letter VII   *Ringmer, Oct. 8, 1770*

To the Hon. Daines Barrington

' . . . A land tortoise, which has been kept for thirty years in a little walled court belonging to the house where I now am visiting, retires under ground about the middle of *November*, and comes forth again about the middle of *April*. When it first appears in the spring it discovers very little inclination towards food ; but in the height of summer grows voracious : and then as the summer declines it's appetite declines ; so that for the last six weeks in autumn it hardly eats at all. Milky plants, such as lettuces, dandelions, sowthistles, are it's favourite dish. In a neighbouring village one was kept till by tradition it was supposed to be an hundred years old. An instance of vast longevity in such a poor reptile ! '

April 12, 1772
                                              To the Hon. Daines Barrington

' Dear Sir,

While I was in *Sussex* last autumn my residence was at
the village near *Lewes*, from whence I had formerly the
pleasure of writing to you.   On the first of *November* I
remarked that the old tortoise, formerly mentioned, began
first to dig the ground in order to the forming of it's
hybernaculum, which it had fixed on just beside a great
tuft of hepaticas.   It scrapes out the ground with it's fore-
feet, and throws it up over it's back with it's hind ; but
the motion of it's legs is ridiculously slow, little exceeding
the hour-hand of a clock ; and suitable to the composure
of an animal said to be a whole month in performing one
feat of copulation.   Nothing can be more assiduous than
this creature night and day in scooping the earth, and
forcing it's great body into the cavity ; but, as the noons
of that season proved unusually warm and sunny, it was
continually interrupted, and called forth by the heat in the
middle of the day ; and though I continued there till the
thirteenth of *November*, yet the work remained unfinished.
Harsher weather, and frosty mornings, would have quickened it's operations.   No part of it's behaviour ever struck
me more than the extreme timidity it always expresses with
regard to rain ; for though it has a shell that would secure
it against the wheel of a loaded cart, yet does it discover
as much solicitude about rain as a lady dressed in all her
best attire, shuffling away on the first sprinklings, and
running it's head up in a corner.   If attended to, it becomes
an excellent weather-glass ; for as sure as it walks elate,

and as it were on tiptoe, feeding with great earnestness in a morning, so sure will it rain before night. It is totally a diurnal animal, and never pretends to stir after it becomes dark. The tortoise, like other reptiles, has an arbitrary stomach as well as lungs; and can refrain from eating as well as breathing for a great part of the year. When first awakened it eats nothing; nor again in the autumn before it retires: through the height of the summer it feeds voraciously, devouring all the food that comes in it's way. I was much taken with it's sagacity in discerning those that do it kind offices: for, as soon as the good old lady comes in sight who has waited on it for more than thirty years, it hobbles towards it's benefactress with aukward alacrity; but remains inattentive to strangers. Thus not only ' *the ox knoweth his owner, and the ass his master's crib*,' but the most abject reptile and torpid of beings distinguishes the hand that feeds it, and is touched with the feelings of gratitude !

I am, etc., etc.

P.S. In about three days after I left *Sussex* the tortoise retired into the ground under the hepatica.'

Letter XVII   *Ringmer, near Lewes, Dec. 9, 1773*
To the Hon. Daines Barrington

' . . . The old tortoise, that I have mentioned in a former letter, still continues in this garden; and retired under ground about the twentieth of *November*, and came out again for one day on the thirtieth: it lies now buried in a wet swampy border under a wall facing to the south, and is enveloped at present in mud and mire !'

Letter XXXVI   *Selborne, Nov. 22, 1777*
                              To the Hon. Daines Barrington

' Dear Sir,

You cannot but remember that the twenty-sixth and twenty-seventh of last *March* were very hot days ; so sultry that everybody complained and were restless under those sensations to which they had not been reconciled by gradual approaches.

This sudden summer-like heat was attended by many summer coincidences ; for on those two days the thermometer rose to sixty-six in the shade ; many species of insects revived and came forth ; some bees swarmed in this neighbourhood ; the old tortoise, near Lewes, in *Sussex*, awakened and came forth out of its dormitory ; and, what is most to my present purpose, many *house-swallows* appeared and were very alert in many places, and particularly at *Cobham*, in *Surrey*.

But as that short warm period was succeeded as well as preceded by harsh severe weather, with frequent frosts and ice, and cutting winds, the insects withdrew, the tortoise retired again into the ground and the swallows were seen no more until the tenth of *April*, when, the rigour of the spring abating, a softer season began to prevail.

Again ; it appears by my journals for many years past, that *house-martins* retire, to a bird, about the beginning of *October* ; so that a person not very observant of such matters would conclude that they had taken their last farewell : but then it may be seen in my diaries also that considerable flocks have discovered themselves again in the first week of *November*, and often on the fourth day of that month only *for one day*; and that not as if they were in actual migration, but playing about at their leisure and feeding calmly, as if no enterprize of moment at all agitated their spirits. And this was the case in the beginning of this very month; for, on the fourth of *November*, more than twenty house-martins, which, in appearance, had all departed about the seventh of *October*, were seen again, for that *one morning only*, sporting between my fields and *the Hanger*, and feasting on insects which swarmed in that sheltered district. The preceding day was wet and blustering, but the fourth was dark and mild, and soft, the wind at south-west, and the thermometer at $50\frac{1}{2}°$; a pitch not common at that season of the year. Moreover, it may not be amiss to add in this place, that whenever the thermometer is above 50 the bat comes flitting out in every autumnal and winter-month.

From all these circumstances laid together, it is obvious that torpid insects, reptiles, and quadrupeds, are awakened from their profoundest slumbers by a little untimely warmth; and therefore that nothing so much promotes this death-like stupor as a defect of heat. And farther, it is reasonable to suppose that two whole species, or at least many individuals of those two species, of *British hirundines*, do never leave this island at all, but partake of the same benumbed state: for we cannot suppose that, after a month's absence, house-martins can return from southern regions to appear for *one* morning in *November*, or that house-swallows should leave the districts of *Africa* to enjoy, in *March*, the transient summer of a *couple* of days.

I am, etc.'

[58]

Letter L   *Selborne, April 21, 1780*
                              To the Hon. Daines Barrington

' Dear Sir,

The old *Sussex* tortoise, that I have mentioned to you so often, is become my property.   I dug it out of it's winter dormitory in *March* last, when it was enough wakened to express it's resentment by hissing ; and, packing it in a box with earth, carried it eighty miles in postchaises.   The rattle and hurry of the journey so perfectly roused it that, when I turned it out on a border, it walked twice down to the bottom of my garden ; however, in the evening, the weather being cold, it buried itself in the loose mould, and continues still concealed.

As it will be under my eye, I shall now have an opportunity of enlarging my observations on it's mode of life, and propensities ; and perceive already that, towards the time of it's coming forth, it opens a breathing place in the ground near it's head, requiring, I conclude, a freer respiration as it becomes more alive.   This creature not only goes under the earth from the middle of *November* to the middle of *April*, but sleeps great part of the summer ; for it goes to bed in the longest days at four in the afternoon, and often does not stir in the morning till late.   Besides, it retires to rest for every shower ; and does not move at all in wet days.

When one reflects on the state of this strange being, it is a matter of wonder to find that Providence should bestow such a profusion of days, such a seeming waste of longevity, on a reptile that appears to relish it so little as to squander more than two thirds of it's existence in a joyless stupor, and be lost to all sensation for months together in the profoundest of slumbers.

While I was writing this letter, a moist and warm afternoon, with the thermometer at 50, brought forth troops of *shell-snails* ; and, at the same juncture, the *tortoise heaved* up the mould, and put out it's head ; and the next morning came forth, as it were raised from the dead ; and walked about till four in the afternoon. This was a curious coincidence ! a very amusing occurrence ! to see such a similarity of feelings between the two *ψερεοιϰει* ! for so the *Greeks* call both the *shell-snail* and the *tortoise*.

Summer birds are, this cold and backward spring, unusually late : I have seen but one swallow yet. This conformity with the weather convinces me more and more that they sleep in the winter.'

More particulars respecting The old Family tortoise.[1]

'Because we call this creature an abject reptile, we are too apt to undervalue his abilities, and depreciate his powers of instinct. Yet he is, as Mr *Pope* says of his lord,

" . . . *much too wise to walk into a well :* "

and has so much discernment as not to fall down an haha ;

[1] G. W. included these particulars as a supplement to *The Antiquities of Selborne*. It is now customary to include them in Letter L. of the *Nat. Hist.*, though comparison with the *Journals* shows them to be inconsistent with its date of April 1780.

but to stop and withdraw from the brink with the readiest precaution.

Though he loves warm weather he avoids the hot sun; because his thick shell, when once heated, would, as the poet says of solid armour—'scald with safety.' He therefore spends the more sultry hours under the umbrella of a large cabbage-leaf, or amidst the waving forests of an asparagus-bed.

But as he avoids heat in the summer, so, in the decline of the year, he improves the faint autumnal beams, by getting within the reflection of a fruit wall: and, though he has never read that planes inclining to the horizon receive a greater share of warmth, he inclines his shell, by tilting it against the wall, to collect and admit every feeble ray.

Pitiable seems the condition of this poor embarrassed reptile: to be cased in a suit of ponderous armour, which he cannot lay aside; to be imprisoned, as it were, within his own shell, must preclude, we should suppose, all activity and disposition for enterprize. Yet there is a season of the year (usually the beginning of June) when his exertions are remarkable. He then walks on tiptoe, and is stirring by five in the morning; and, traversing the garden, examines every wicket and interstice in the fences, through which he will escape if possible: and often has eluded the care of the gardener, and wandered to some distant field. The motives that impel him to undertake these rambles seem to be of the amorous kind: his fancy then becomes intent on sexual attachments, which transport him beyond his usual gravity, and induce him to forget for a time his ordinary solemn deportment.'

APPENDIX 1

Dr Chandler

' DR CHANDLER and Lady, who have been abroad almost four years, and who returned from the continent only last February, have borrowed Selborne parsonage-house for the summer, and came to reside last week. The Dr who is an unsettled man, likes this method of procuring an habitation, because it looks so like *not* settling. Roaming about becomes a habit with Gentry, as well as mendicants ; who, when they have once taken up a strolling life, can never be perswaded to stay at their own parishes. The Lady is very big with child, and sent for her midwife this morning : so they reached Selborne just in time. They brought a little son with them, a pretty boy, who was born at Rolle in Switzerland, as it were by accident, while they were posting home for England. The Dr seems to like his child better, because he is not sure in what kingdom he was begotten, whether at Naples, or at Rome, or at Florence, or where. Rome is the place that the Dr admires, where he can have his fill of *Virtù* : he has, I find, secret languishings to return to that capital ; to study in the Vatican, and to dine with Cardinals.'

G. W. Letter to Samuel Barker, May 6, 1790.

The *Journals* show that Dr Chandler kept a sharp eye on Hirundines during his travels ; taught the White household to make lime-blossom tea ; and bought a pound of English truffles for 2s. 6d.

Tortoises at Ringmer

In a letter to his brother, John White, dated Sept. 26, 1774, Gilbert White remarks:

' When you write to Linn. next, pray talk to him about tortoises. There are tortoises whose shells are always open *behind* and *before* " apertura testae anterior," as he says himself, " pro capite et brachiis; posterior pro cauda et femoribus." These apertures are supported, as it were, by pillars on each side and can *never* be closed. Of such construction is the shell of Mrs Snooke's present *living* tortoise, Timothy. But then there are tortoises whose under shell has a *cardo*, an hinge, about the middle of their bellies, commanding one lid or flap forward, and one lid backward (like the double-lidded snuff-boxes) which when shut conceal the head and legs and tail of the reptile entirely, and keep out all annoyances. Two such (very small they were) Mrs Snooke had formerly; and the shells lie still in her room over the hall.'

Linn. : Linnaeus.

· ✳ ·

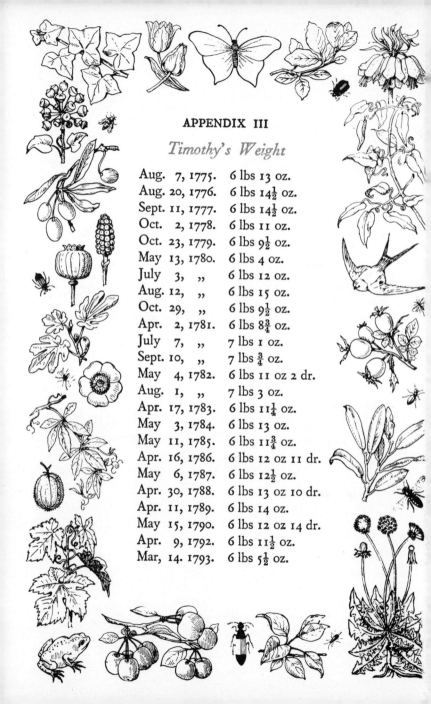

APPENDIX III

Timothy's Weight

Aug. 7, 1775.	6 lbs 13 oz.
Aug. 20, 1776.	6 lbs 14½ oz.
Sept. 11, 1777.	6 lbs 14½ oz.
Oct. 2, 1778.	6 lbs 11 oz.
Oct. 23, 1779.	6 lbs 9½ oz.
May 13, 1780.	6 lbs 4 oz.
July 3, „	6 lbs 12 oz.
Aug. 12, „	6 lbs 15 oz.
Oct. 29, „	6 lbs 9½ oz.
Apr. 2, 1781.	6 lbs 8¾ oz.
July 7, „	7 lbs 1 oz.
Sept. 10, „	7 lbs ¾ oz.
May 4, 1782.	6 lbs 11 oz 2 dr.
Aug. 1, „	7 lbs 3 oz.
Apr. 17, 1783.	6 lbs 11¼ oz.
May 3, 1784.	6 lbs 13 oz.
May 11, 1785.	6 lbs 11¾ oz.
Apr. 16, 1786.	6 lbs 12 oz 11 dr.
May 6, 1787.	6 lbs 12½ oz.
Apr. 30, 1788.	6 lbs 13 oz 10 dr.
Apr. 11, 1789.	6 lbs 14 oz.
May 15, 1790.	6 lbs 12 oz 14 dr.
Apr. 9, 1792.	6 lbs 11½ oz.
Mar, 14. 1793.	6 lbs 5½ oz.